Walking *with the* Lord

WHAT A WAY TO GO

Walking with the Lord

What A Way To Go

BEVERLY K. PLAUCHÉ

ReadersMagnet, LLC

WALKING WITH THE LORD – WHAT A WAY TO GO
Copyright © 2022 by Beverly K. Plauché

Published in the United States of America
ISBN   Paperback: 978-1-959165-04-0
ISBN   eBook: 978-1-959165-05-7

All rights reserved. No part of this publication may be reproduced, stored in a retrieval system or transmitted in any way by any means, electronic, mechanical, photocopy, recording or otherwise without the prior permission of the author except as provided by USA copyright law.

The opinions expressed by the author are not necessarily those of ReadersMagnet, LLC.

ReadersMagnet, LLC
10620 Treena Street, Suite 230 | San Diego, California, 92131 USA
1.619. 354. 2643 | www.readersmagnet.com

Book design copyright © 2022 by ReadersMagnet, LLC. All rights reserved.

Cover design by Kent Gabutin
Interior design by Dorothy Lee

My life started out pretty normal. I was given two parents that loved me and a sister that was quite a challenge. I won't get into that. Well, if you really have to know here's the story. When I was six months old and my sister was 3 ½, my mother had put me out in the driveway in my stroller. When she checked on me, I was gone. She noticed that the garage door had been open but now was closed. When she opened the garage door there was my sister with an assortment of tools (screw drivers, hammers, and pliers) and in her hand was a saw. She was getting ready to cut off my arm. Wow! Mom caught her just in time. God really was in control even if I didn't know it.

I was raised in church from the time I was born. My family went to church on Sunday morning, Sunday night, and Wednesday night. We all sang in the choir, went to church socials and my sister and I participated in church competitions. My sister and I went to church camp for ten years. You would have thought we would have gotten the picture. But you see all that stuff did not make us a God loving family. We never talked about God. We never discussed his character, his love, his ways, or his sovereignty. We never discussed why we shouldn't do certain things. We were just told not to do them. I did gain a lot of knowledge about God over the eighteen years, but the knowledge was just the facts. It was nothing but the facts. Oh how I thought I truly believed in God. Sometimes, when

I would pray, I would see Jesus on the cross. I would cry in sorrow for him. How realistic is that! There was no doubt in my mind that God and Jesus existed. The problem was, even the demons believe in God and Jesus. Mark 1:23-24 explains. A man possessed by a demon was present and began shouting, "Why are you bothering us, Jesus of Nazareth—have you come to destroy us demons: I know who you are—the Holy Son of God!"

There was something definitely wrong! The facts in my head had not moved to my heart. I didn't know how to move this wealth of information to my heart and didn't even know I needed to. I lived life the way I wanted to with no regard for what God thought. I lied to get what I wanted and I didn't think there was anything wrong with having sex before marriage. I was a mess.

I was always overweight. I kept putting on more and more pounds. I never dated in high school; therefore, I thought I would never have the chance to get married. When I was nineteen, I finally met a man on a blind date. His name was Wayne Hansen. I didn't have expectations for any man, so he fit the bill. The problem was that he had mental problems, he was always looking to take advantage of a situation or people, and he was an agnostic. I went to striptease joints with him and drank hurricanes and other concoctions. I wondered why I was going to striptease joints but kept on going. I had the thought that I would rather my boyfriend go with me than go by himself and maybe pick up another woman. How Godly is that?

I met Wayne 40 years ago. Wayne had a daughter, Lynn by his first marriage and he had custody of her. I was in college at the time. I told you I lied when I needed to, so I did not tell my parents that he was divorced. I was lying by omission. One Sunday at the dinner table I was telling my parents about my friend that was dating a divorced man. My father turned to Wayne and said "You've haven't been married before have you"? Wayne said, "Yes I have". I left the table and heard footsteps behind me. It was Mom. She said, "Well, he doesn't have children does he". I said, "Yes, he does." On came the war. My father was none to happy that I was dating a divorced man. He and Mom loved Wayne's daughter but they never accepted Wayne.

About six months had transpired and Wayne and I decided to get married. We picked out a ring and everything. My dad never drank very much, but the night we told him we were getting married, he was drinking a lot. He told me that, if we got married, he would not pay for my college education. That night I could not sleep. I tossed and turned and was very confused. The next morning, Wayne came over and was telling me all the things we could do with the additional money I would be making. I thought all he wants me for is money. At that point, I said, "I will not marry you right now, we will have to wait until I graduate. I did not realize it but, God had given me those confused feelings. He knew that it was best if I finished school. I have had two careers. The second is a school teacher which I could not have acquired as easy without my business degree. Thank goodness God is in control all the time. That's what's neat about God, he watches out for us even when we're not walking with him. When I graduated, Wayne and I got married. Since Wayne had custody of Lynn, she lived with us. Her biological mother didn't come to see her very much. Since she didn't show much responsibility with her, I didn't want her Mother to take her for visits. Her biological mom had six more children with several different men, so it was good that she was not around her much. God was even looking out for us then and once again we didn't even know it. Lynn was a very loving child. After we got married, she went back to school and said her mommy and daddy got married. Even though she was glad to have a mother, I was definitely not the type of mother I should have been. I wanted to, I just failed. I wouldn't let her have chocolate milk, a night light, and sometimes I spanked her with a belt. How terrible was that.

I was also greedy. I got Beanie Weanies at salvage sales and made her eat them every day. To this day, she will not eat food like that. I love her very much, but I didn't always know how to show her. I guess she has continued to overlook my shortcomings. Along with the bad, I did learn to meet her needs and we developed a close bond through the years.

I did take her to church with me. I tried to train her in God's ways, but how could I teach her when I didn't know myself. The neat thing about God is that he had his hand on us the entire time.

Even though I wasn't walking with the Lord, I always wanted Wayne to go to church with me, but he was very stubborn. He said all Christians were hypocrites. It was an uphill climb. I finally talked him into going to church and he realized that maybe he was wrong. Wayne would flirt with my church friends and make me feel really bad. One time I found some papers in which he was writing a story about him and his girlfriend riding in a red convertible. In the story, I was the terrible wife. What little self-esteem I had went to pot.

After Wayne and I had been married for seven years, I lost sixty five pounds. I WAS A NEW PERSON ON THE OUTSIDE BUT THE SAME PERSON ON THE INSIDE. I received attention from other men that I had never imagined. One of the men at work came on to me. Since I didn't know what it was like with anyone else, I decided to play around with him. I was never emotionally attached to him and I'm glad of that. I was also having sex with another man, but once again I never got emotionally attached. Wayne had it in his mind that he wanted to have businesses in which he could sit back and rake in the money. I never liked that idea. It was so risky. Every time he got the chance, he went for it. When we first got married, Wayne wanted his x-in-laws to raise chickens. He would buy the chickens, chicken coups, and food. They would do the rest. He bought everything they needed and they did take care of the chickens. When the chickens were old enough to start laying eggs, they decided it was too much work. Everything we put into the business was gone. I told you before that I liked money. It was very important to have money in the bank. That little fiasco did not fit well with me.

My parents lived near Athens. The city had a Black Eye Pea Festival every year. Wayne had gotten interested in silk screening T Shirts. Thought he could make a lot of money. He developed 3 designs for T shirts and then had them made. Here is the problem. The designs he developed were pathetic. One of the T Shirts had Acropolis A Crop of Peas on it. The other two were not that bad, but still bad. We did not know until we arrived at the festival, that Waylon Jennings and Willie Nelson would be singing. All we would've had to do was put something about the two men on the T

Shirts and they would have sold like hot cakes. Wayne just did not do all his investigation. He bought 4,000 T Shirts and we did not sell many. He had borrowed $2000 from my Dad which he never paid back. After that, Dad learned his lesson. He never loaned Wayne any money anymore.

Do you think that, at this point, Wayne learned his lesson NO, NO, NO, NO, NO. When we sold our house, Wayne received $22,000. We bought a house. Did Wayne pay a down payment on the house? NO. He purchased a condo. Did he pay a down payment on the condo? NO. He could not rent the condo and lost money every day. Here is the big one. He purchased an ice cream shop. I had just lost 65 pounds and he bought an ice cream shop. That was very devastating to me. I love hot fudge sundaes. Could I keep from eating them? NO. Did I gain all the weight back? No. I was determined never to gain all the weight back. Did he pay a down payment on the ice cream shop? No. He borrowed the entire amount $20,000. Here's what happened. The manager of the ice cream shop quit. Wayne was trying to run the business and work at an accounting job at the same time. Did that work? No. He was fired. Could he pay his bills? No. He came to me one day and said he would be leaving town. He was afraid he would be arrested for not paying his $20,000 bill. He left with a broken down car and a tent. I was not upset. I was relieved. After ten years in a roller coaster marriage, I was free. Once again, God knew what he was doing.

Wayne and I got divorced and Lynn went with me. Wayne and his x-wife gave me rights to finish raising her. What a miracle. That made the ten year ridiculous marriage worth it to me.

After the divorce was complete, I found out I was five months pregnant. When I told Lynn, I was pregnant; she said "We've got a lot of work to do". How precious is that coming from a fifteen year old girl? Lynn even collected money from relatives and bought me a round baby bed. It was just what I wanted.

Krista came on the scene and was a precious baby. I wasn't worried that she wouldn't know her biological father. At this time, I didn't think of the affect this situation might have on Krista. I had just had a baby and enjoyed every moment. I always said that

Wayne was the Daddy so I never knew of any negative implications from the birth. I made the most of it. Lynn and I enjoyed Krista very much. Dressing her up, putting bows on her head, and showing her off. The bows would not stay in her hair. What a problem!! I decided to use toothpaste. One day as we were in the car, I heard smack, smack, smack. I turned around and Krista was eating her bow. That was the end of the toothpaste era. Lynn and I continued doing all the things you do with a baby. We loved her with our whole hearts but, I still didn't think about the hurt that Krista would have to go through because she didn't know her dad.

Lynn was a strong willed girl. She had a boyfriend, she was in flag core and she was enjoying her high school years. The problem was that she was very, very smart and had never been given the chance to show it. She missed too many days of school and was kicked out. (That's how they did it in the olden days). I tried to get her into another school, but we could not out smart those principles. She ended up doing everything but graduate. She received her GED. She decided to go to junior college and made a 4.0 average. I told you she was smart. She was accepted to Baylor University and received her Tax Accounting degree. What a success story! Don't ever think your kids cannot achieve what they want to achieve. Now we are at *Phase* 2 of my life. This phase is God driven, exciting, emotional, and anything else you can think of. What could have been a desperate and miserable attempt to raise a baby and a 15 year old girl all by myself, turned into a God given life of hope, love, and, opportunities.

When Krista was six months old, I decided to start reading the Bible. I was praying that I would meet a man that would sit with me in church. That's all I thought I wanted. At this point in my life, I was beginning to look to God instead of myself. I was stepping out in faith and decided to go to my home church in Oak Cliff, a part of Dallas, Texas. I started going the next Sunday. Don, my future husband, also showed up that day. I was holding Krista and looking at a calendar of events. Don walked up and said, "Hello". I responded and that was it. I had a ring on my finger and was holding a six month old baby. He thought I was married. To my surprise I later found out that Don had been praying for a wife for 7 years. He would meet girls and date them, but things never worked out. He was a Catholic and had decided at 12 years old that he wanted to do something for God. He thought about being a priest but didn't think he could live in celibacy.

The next Sunday I went to the singles class. Who do you think was there? Don. He looked surprised and said, "I thought you were married". I said, "No", I'm divorced. Then he asked the obvious question, "Would you ever go back to him? I said <u>NOOOOOOOOOOOOOOOOOO.</u> He then asked if he could sit with me in church. My prayer had been answered. God had made a way for me. But there was a lot more to come**. Keep reading**. There was something else that made this meeting a miracle. Don didn't have a car and he was attending the Assembly of God College in Waxahachie which was about 30 miles away. The chances of our meeting at the same time and place were very slim. But, of course, God was in it. We started dating and had wonderful times.

But, how does a person know they are dating a Godly man? I noticed that Don was excited about God. He talked a lot about God on our first date. He knew things that only God could have told him. He also helped me get excited about God. Don was 33 years old and wanted a wife very much. But, he only wanted the women that God wanted him to have. From the Biblical point of view, I was not the women for Don. I was divorced, had 2 children, 15 and 6 months, and I had had several affairs. I definitely was not a Godly woman. I was not born again yet, but at first, Don didn't realize that. Some people were telling Don to leave that divorced person along. Don was confused. We got along and were having a great time so Don decided to pray, for 3 days, about our relationship and wanted God to show him if he should continue in our relationship. He came over after the 3 day period and this is what he said. "God said he misses you." It's hard to explain. It was just like God was talking to me face to face. That one statement changed my belief in God from my head to my heart.

I found something that Don had written concerning this situation and thought it might give you some incite into what Don was facing.

"When I met you, Bev, I was a very hurt person and prayed for a friend. I wanted just a friend to talk to and share with and for some reason, God called you to do it. I really never thought we could be more than friends. I was taught that a person that was single should not marry a divorced person. I tried as hard as I could to get out of the relationship. I didn't know why, but for some reason it seemed that I couldn't. I had an idea in my mind of who I should get involved with and didn't think it was you. I prayed and prayed and the Holy Spirit always sent me back to you. I prayed one last time and really felt that you were the one to marry. I decided against the religious traditions that seem to say, Don't marry a divorced women. It was difficult for me. The religiosity of the Bible had you stamped, but the wisdom of the Holy Spirit saw your real desire to become an intense devoted Christian. The Holy Spirit saw through to your heart. I saw potential, but it was clouded. I had the wisdom to follow the Holy Spirit. He began to strip away the clouds."

If you are looking for a husband, no matter if your divorced or single, always wait for a Godly man.

When we were first married, Don told me that I was not meeting some of his needs. But before he told me, he prayed about it. He told me that the Holy Spirit had shown him that only God could meet those needs. I never heard another word from Don about that subject. What could have been a terrible fight with ongoing connotations became a peaceful time. Don had an anger problem and it was in his family. As I learned more and more about God, I thought I had the answer for his anger. I told him that, when he first felt anger, he needed not to give in to it. He shouldn't let it sink to his soul. If he did give in to it, it would become a hook for Satan to use against him. He wouldn't listen, he kept cutting me off. I was so mad I was crying. That didn't even have an affect on Don. We ended the conversation. The next day when Don got home, he wanted to talk to me. He said that God had shown him that I was right about his anger and he needed to listen to me sometime. God said that I had been like a weed but now I was like flower. That surely touched my heart. I had to take the good with the bad. One time God showed Don that I had a self righteous spirit and needed to get rid of it or there would be consequences. I started working on my self righteous spirit right then.

I didn't understand how Don could hear from God. I said, "How do you do that? "God just gives me thoughts" he said. Not an audible voice, just thoughts. One day, Don called me at work and told me that God told him that I was going to get a $300 a month raise in October. I received a $650 a month raise right in October. He also knew things about other people that only God could have told him. One Sunday we went to my Mom and Dad's church. We were the only ones that showed up in the Sunday School Class except the teacher. Don began to talk to her about the situation between her husband and her. She said that Don was right on. God continued to show Don things until I could understood that Don really could hear from God. I now knew that I could trust Don and he was truly a Godly man.

There was one hang up. Isn't there always hang-ups. There's one good thing about God. He can turn hang-ups into wonderful things. The professors at the college were saying, "Leave that divorced women alone." Don was confused because we really liked each other. Don and I couldn't understand why God would allow a man, who had prayed for a wife for 7 years and never been married and a divorced woman with 2 children, to even like each other. We decided that only God knew why and he was the sovereign God and the only one to make that decision. Even the fact that I had been unfaithful to my first husband didn't faze Don. He knew that God always gives everyone second chances. After all this confusion, Don told me there was only one thing to do. **_Pray._** He decided to pray, for three days, concerning the continuation of our relationship. He came over at the end of this period and told me what God had said. God said, "He misses you". I thought Wow! **_God misses me!_** That's what changed my heart.

The heart change is what has to happen in everyone's life in order to live for God and be saved. Would you like to know what happens when your heart changes? Here it is. We all have a spirit. Even unbelievers agree that we all have a spirit. What they don't know is that our spirits can either be alive or dead. When we are born, all of our spirits are dead. Why? Because of Adam and Eve's sin. Adam and Eve had no sin until Satan came in and changed it for everyone. Through Adam and Eve's sin, everyone is born with a dead spirit causing there to be no relationship with God. The Holy Spirit does not live in unbelievers' heart. The Holy Spirit is our comforter (in time of trouble) and shows us ways in which we need to change. The Holy Spirit is our connection to God. He's the one who gives us God's thoughts and ideas. In an unbeliever, there is no conviction for sin. Unbelievers do what they want, when they want and how they want just as I did. A person doesn't know it, but they're not truly happy when they live that way.

If your spirit is reborn through your decision to accept Jesus as your savior, You think of things differently, and you want to change from the way you did things to a new way of doing them. It just comes naturally. Now that my spirit was alive, I began to combine the knowledge in my head with my new spirit. You will now see what wonderful things God can do with your new heart and spirit.

It's not as easy as it sounds until you learn to let God do his thing. Over the years, I had built up walls in my soul that I didn't even know about. I was so proud of myself because I never got depressed and then I realized I was never really happy. My emotions were always in neutral. I was never happy or sad. I didn't realize what I was missing until I met Don and saw the joy of love and life that he had. You see I had a lot of garbage and stinky stuff in me that needed to be destroyed and thrown away. Don described me as:

    Self serving

    Driven

    Short sighted

    Opinionated – I was always right

    Money hungry

    Socially aloof – I thought talking was a waste of time

    Loner

I did have some good points. I just didn't know what they were. Usually changes don't happen over night. You see God wants permanent changes. Sometimes that requires daily life experiences and trials that get rid of our bad character traits. It also requires changes in the normal way we carry on our daily lives. God doesn't want us to think how we would do things, but how he would do it. If we don't know how to do it his way, all we have to do is **_pray_**. Does that mean we will always get an obvious answer? **_NO_**. If we don't get an answer from God, we go in the direction we think God wants us to until he changes our path. We keep praying and believing that we will get an answer. God works so differently with each one of us that we never know exactly how he will work it out. But there's one thing for sure. He always works it out. He told me one time **"I may not snatch you out, but I will get you through it**." How much better can it get. God, the creator of the universe, is right there with you every step of the way. Does that mean it will always go your way? **_NO._** You will find out that God's ways are always better than our ways even if it hurts.

Plauché Family

Brad and Don

Along our way, God provided Don and me with a wonderful baby boy. We had three children now. Lynn had married, but she is still mine. Blood is not thicker than water. Krista was three and ½. We had our full family now.

I worked for Stokely Van Camp/Quaker Oats for 22 years. I definitely had my ups and downs. When I met Don, he told me that God was going to build my character at work and God didn't waste any time getting started. In my job I had to answer the phone a lot. People had a lot of questions and it was my responsibility to answer them or find the answer. I had a lot of self pity. I thought I was overworked and never got the job done. I had more to do than I could complete in a day and always had things left over. I would answer the phone in a way that would make people feel sorry they were calling me. That had a huge impact on the people I was talking to. If they didn't feel bad before calling me, they surely felt bad afterwards. Don called one day and said, "Bev, I can't believe you answer the phone that way. That remark made me sit up and take notice. I began to answer the phone with a happy voice. I began projecting a happiness I didn't feel. Then, as time progressed,

I realized that I was a hypocrite. I was projecting something that I was not. What did I do? **_Pray_**. I asked the Lord to help me feel the joy I was missing. I kept projecting joy and never gave up hope. One day as I was walking into work, I started laughing with a hearty, energetic, true joy. I thought to myself, Wow, that's **_God._** He is giving me his joy and happiness. I asked God to leave me just a little bit of the joy. To this day, he has left me with his supernatural joy. Don began calling me Bubble Box Beverly.

As office manager, I had done what I pleased with little direction for 7 years and with quite a bit of success. Payroll, accounts payable, finished goods, raw materials inventory all ran smooth. We would have corporate audits and we never had any big hits. When Quaker Oats bought the company suddenly that came to an end. The Plant Manager couldn't stand me and his assistant told me he didn't think I could do the job. You've got to realize, at this point, my job was more important to me than God or family. Long hours (one time I worked 22 hours to get payroll done) and no energy led me to become a shell of a woman who was not willing to give up. I loved status, authority, and power—worldly that is. I enjoyed business trips, being important, and expense reports. Seven years later, I was told that my department and another were being consolidated and I would loose my managerial job. At least I would still have a job even if it would be a lower one. The good thing is, I still got the same pay. Isn't God so good.

That had to be the hardest thing I had ever faced. To be an unemotional person, I sure cried a lot. I had a lot of vain imaginations. 2 Corinthians 10:5 says "Casting down imaginations, and every high thing that exalted itself against the knowledge of God, and bringing into captivity every thought to the obedience of Jesus Christ". Some of my imaginations were: You won't go on any more trips or have any more expense reports. You won't be able to tell people what to do anymore. That was the big one! Luckily, I realized that God wanted to change me and I knew that pride and status were the big issues. I wish I had a penny for every time I the bound the spirit of pride or rejected a negative thought. You see it's the choices we make that turns the tide. I could have let those negative thoughts embellish me. I could have thought on them over and over again. I learned through experience that the quicker you let them go and don't give in, the better off you will be. The second I had a negative thought, I would cast it out of my mind. I would not allow it to sink to my soul. If it did, it would be a hook for Satan to use against me. By the way, it took 6 or 7 months for those thoughts to go away. You see, Satan is tough. He can hang in there for a long time. We just have to be persistent because, with God's help, we can outlast him. God showed me that even though in the physical world I was a failure, spiritually I was a success. That made a difference for me. The physical world didn't matter to me anymore. God showed Don that even though my worldly status and authority were being crushed, he was building my spiritual status and authority. For the first time, I understood about the house built on the rock or sand. I was so practical that all I could see was a house being rained on. But, then I saw that the things we go through make our spiritual foundation stronger each time. Matthew 7: 24-27 Jesus says, "Therefore whosoever heareth these sayings of mine, and doest them, I will liken him unto a wise man, which built his house on a rock: And the rain descended, and the floods came, and the winds blew, and beat upon that house; and it fell not: for it was founded upon a rock. An every one that heareth these sayings of mine, and doeth them not, shall be likened unto a foolish man, which built his rock on the sand: And the rain descended and the floods came, and the winds blew, and beat upon the house, and it fell: and great was the fall of it, God showed me that if I could maintain the right attitude he could make me happy doing anything. At this point, I decided to put my career in God's hands. How safe is that. Some of us don't realized how safe God is, but he is the safest place for us. He knows us better than we know ourselves. He knows what is going to happen to us every second of every day, so why shouldn't we give him a chance? I could've gone out and gotten another managerial job, but would that obtain the results that God wanted? I told God that I would stay at Quaker, do whatever they wanted me to do, with a good attitude, until God opened a window for me to quit.

With my new job, I had one more obstacle at Quaker. There was a man whom I thought could not do the job. I thought he was not organized, didn't do things when he should, and guess what happened. He became my boss. **<u>Oh! No!</u>** What was I to do. All I could do was stay, pray, and love that man. My new job was the same job I had had when I first came to work at Stokley Van Camp. One day he called me in the office and started telling me everything I was doing wrong. I just sat there and said OK, OK, OK. I did not understand what I was doing wrong but, I remembered the time Jesus was before the Pharisees and he didn't argue with them either. So I just kept my mouth shut. By the way, I never heard from him again. What a miracle.

When I got laid off, I remember thinking, "This is too good to be true". What is going on"? "When will I start being tormented"? Guess what happened, I never had any bad thoughts or bad feelings. Satan had learned that he cannot always run over me. That doesn't mean he didn't keep trying. It was as if God had a protective umbrella over my soul and spirit and it was great.

My driven spirit would naturally want to go right back to work. I would be getting severance pay plus my new job's pay. God had changed me so much that I didn't even have a desire to do that. I had been offered a job as, Office Manager, there in Dallas with the same money and status as before, but my family was more important. I just wanted to stay home with them and enjoy my time off. Thank God, he had turned my thinking around.

Let's now go back. When my heart was changed, I began wanting to hear from God like Don did. What did I do? **<u>Pray!</u>** I told God that he gave Don a dissertation and I just wanted a little bit of what he gave Don. I also had the desire to do a study on your soul. I found out that your soul is your **mind, will** and **emotions**. **<u>Wow!</u>** If your soul is your mind, well that's how God gives you thoughts. What a treasure! That's how God does it. Guess who else can give you thoughts? The devil. Both God and the devil gave me thoughts at Quaker and I was getting better at discerning the two.

Before Don and I got married, he found out that Lynn was her own person which caused a few problems. One day, Don said "Let's go pray for Lynn. We prayed for her and soon after I had this thought, "**Just show Lynn love.**" I thought, how can I, I'm mad at her. I totally ignored the thought and went on with my life.

Two weeks later Don said "Let's go pray for Lynn. We went and prayed for her and I got that same thought, **Just show Lynn love."** I was amazed and realized that God had given me that thought. I wouldn't ever have thought that on my own because I was expecting Lynn to change not me. When God shows me something, I would immediately act on it. I called Lynn and told her I loved her. The next time I saw her, we hugged and kissed. I'm not a huggy or kissy person but I did it anyway. It was nice!! God is an unconditional God and he had shown me the same concept. I may not have liked what Lynn was doing, but I still loved her.

My life really changed at that point. I had really heard from God. It was like he was right in front of me even though I couldn't see him. God wants to be right there with us and for us. There are many ways God can reveal things to us. Some of the ways are God's thoughts, the Bible, and other people's confirmations of what we've heard from God. God is so creative he likes to do things different with different people.

Don's description of me as a loner hit the nail right on the head. The first thing God did was to put me in a position to reach out to people. Let's see how he did it. I was sitting in church, minding my own business. At the end of church I had this thought "Ask her if she needs a prayer partner". He was speaking of the lady sitting next to me whom I had never met. I wanted to say "God, have you lost your mind"? "I don't even introduce myself to strangers and you want to ask her if she needs a prayer partner." How did I know that God was giving me that idea? It was an instruction. I don't give myself instructions like that!!! I would never have thought to do that. Not in a million years. When God gives me an idea, I say to myself "How fast can I do it". This was only the second time God had given me a thought, but it was special no matter what the thought was. I was so nervous. I thought she might let me have it. But when you are doing something for God, it has to be OK even if you think it won't. You see it doesn't matter what the world thinks, it only matters what God thinks. When you step out for God, your setting you rewards in Heaven even if it doesn't go the way you think it will here on earth. I did ask her and she said she had been praying for a prayer partner. Boy was I relieved. This lady was from Brazil. I love people from other cultures and accents. This experience would be quite a treasure to me. God sure knew what he was doing.

We exchanged phone numbers and talked on the phone. One night she called and said she really needed to talk to me. She came over and began to tell me that she was just realizing that she had been sexually abused as a child most of her life. She thought she had multiple personalities and was on the verge of a nervous breakdown. I went to her counselor with her. There was something funny. There was a cross with Jesus on it, but we never prayed or even talked about how God could help out in this situation. The first night she was explaining why she had tried to commit suicide. It was the first time she remembered. That was a huge thing for her. The next time we went, she explained that she was three years old and in a pretty white dress and he was chasing her. I was gripping my chair and praying a lot. I decided at that point to get her some other help. I contacted my church and found out that the nursery director had dealt with child abuse. They set up a meeting and helped the lady realize what she was going through. The most important thing was that God loved her. She started crying when she realized that God loved her anyway.

One Sunday Christine walked up to me and she was trembling. She said in class the teacher was explaining that we are all conquerors. The devil immediately told her she would never be anything. We went to the back room and took authority in Jesus blood over any demon that was attacking her. In church she was praising the Lord. We do not have to give into Satan. He has to leave in Jesus name.

Christine was married to a man and it was not a happy marriage. She decided to leave him. She was living with a woman who was on illegal drugs. She surely didn't need to be in that situation. She decided to move in with us. Don, Brad, Krista, myself, and Christine were living in a 3 bedroom mobile home. The wonderful thing about this is that when it's God's will that something happen, it will work out. Brad's new room was in the corner of the living room. We never felt crowded or scrunched. She lived with us for a while which provided time for her healing. She ended up getting married. Don gave her away, Krista was the flower girl, Brad was the ring bearer, and I was the mother of the bride. Needless to say, that experience knocked down a couple of my walls. I now realized how important relationships really are.

One day I was sitting in church and a lady walked up to my aisle. I did not know her either. I had the idea to ask her to sit by me. Luckily this was not as hard as the first time I received instructions from the Holy Spirit. We got to know each other. I would go to her house and talk. She was just discovering that her husband was having an affair. We talked and prayed and talked and prayed and talked and prayed. Once again, I enjoyed something that was not natural to me. God is good all the time!!

As you can see, God took me, a person who never introduced myself to a stranger, was an observer, and thought talking was a waste of time, and turned me into a person who is drawn to people and who almost never hesitates when meeting a new face.

Just remember when you have a thought which is totally opposite to your normal way of thinking and it's positive and good, it might be God. Just do it. You never know what can happen.

Early in my Christian life, Don told me I was going to be anointed by God. I didn't know exactly what he meant, when it would happen or how I would respond. I did know that Don could hear from God and he wouldn't lead me astray. One Sunday I went to church by myself. We would always get in groups and pray. I said to myself, I wasn't going to pray with anyone since I was by myself. Always be careful of what you think because God may have other ideas. There was a couple kind of close to me and when we found prayer partners, no one went to them. I walked over to them and asked if they needed prayer. The man said yes we want to be saved. Wow! You could have knocked me over with a feather. I hadn't prayed the salvation prayer with many people, but I jumped right in and prayed with them for their salvation. All I can say is Wow! Wow! Wow!

Don did not like our mobile home. While Don was praying, God told Don that he wanted him to have a house we could work on so that we could get a lot for a little. Don did not have much experience working on things, but God told him he would send people to help. I remember praying and telling God I didn't want to work all day and come home and work on the house all night. I told God I would, I just didn't want to. One Wednesday night we were at church. The Holy Spirit told Don to pray a covenant pray for our house with that lady over there. Don nor I knew the lady. When we introduced ourselves, she said she was a real estate agent. Isn't that just the way God does things. We told her that we were to pray with her and what we wanted. She told us that houses like that didn't open up very often, but she would call us if it did. God is so punctual that, right when I got laid off and was no longer tied to Dallas, the lady called and told us there was a house in Frost that might serve our purpose. We immediately saw the house and guess what, it didn't need any repairs right away. There was another pray answered.

Don and I did not have jobs. So there was no way to buy the house. God told Don "As long as the window is barely open, keep going in that direction." That's exactly what we did. We leased the house for one year and then purchased it. It is now paid for. What a blessing!!!!!!!!!!!!!!!!

When we moved to Frost, Krista had been in Christian schools all her life and now Don was home schooling her. She made good grades, but never did well on National tests. I asked her teacher and she said some kids are like that. I prayed that Krista would be able to remember what she learned. I did not ask for her to make A's. When we got to Frost, Krista was put in the lower class. I thought she was smarter than that and tried to talk her into going to a more academic class. She refused, but her teachers thought the same thing and they talked her into moving. Krista just flew and did great. She even became valedictorian of her senior class. Please, never give up on your kids.

During our marriage, Don and I struggled with finances. It wasn't a problem because, God always provided a way. Sometimes, Don and I didn't realize that it **wasn't hard.** The process of learning how to deal with unfortunate circumstances in a spiritual way is the key. Each time we were in a hard spot we prayed and asked for God's help. We always received God's answers in different ways. Sometimes slow sometimes fast. Answered pray was always in God's time. That's where patience comes in. When I was laid off from Quaker Oats, we didn't have money for car repairs or health insurance. I decided to pray that we would have God's protection. I knew that God could decide to throw in a monkey wrench along the way, but I had faith in God to take care of us. This faith came from God. One day God told me ***"I may not snatch you out of it, but I will get you through it".*** How special is that. I knew that even if I had to go through something that was really, really, really bad, God would be there to hold my hand. God has a way of turning bad into good. Jeremiah 29:11-13 says "For I know the thoughts that I think toward you, saith the Lord, thoughts of peace, and not of evil, to give you an expected end. Then shall ye call upon me, and ye shall go and pray unto me, and I will harken unto you. And ye shall seek me, and find me, when ye shall search for me with your whole heart." In the area of my car, God did many miracles. I had prayed that if I had car trouble, I would be in a spot that I could get help and no one would take advantage of me or hurt me. One day I was driving and stopped to use the phone. When I got out of the car, I saw that I had a flat tire. A filling station was a much better place to get help than on the highway. One day I was driving into my driveway. At that very moment, my water pump went out. One day I was driving past a friend from church's house and the transmission in my car went out. I was in the middle of the road. A friend helped me move my car out of the road. Isn't God good?

One day, my son's side was hurting. I knew we had to take him to the doctor. We didn't have a doctor in Frost and no insurance so we took him to a hospital in Dallas. Brad did have appendicitis. He got through the surgery just fine. My husband had called the billing department three times to try and find out how we could pay the $5000 bill. As God would do it, someone paid our bill. We never knew who did it, but we did know that God was in it all the time.

Don and I had a lot of financial problems because he could never get a teaching certificate. He tried three times, but something always blew up in his face. You see, Satan did not want Don to be a success in the physical world. Satan did not want Don to have the ministry that God wanted him to have. When we first met, Don decided to leave the college he was going to and attend another college to become a teacher. He received his degree, but not his teacher's certificate. He went to work for a private school, but realized the pay was not enough for our family.

When we first met, Don asked me if I was willing to have a ministry for the Lord. This was before my heart was changed, but I thought that God was so neat I would love to have a ministry for Him. Don said he wanted to have a ministry in a French speaking country. Where do you think I thought we would minister? I thought we would minister in France, of course. His grandmother spoke fluent French and Don being from Louisiana was of Cajun French decent. Don majored in French in college and could speak it quite well. We knew the ultimate goal was a French speaking country, but did not know how to get there or where we would be going. About seven years after we got married, I had grown in leaps and bounds with the Lord. The experiences I had gone through and our ability to hear the Lord's thoughts had given us a big punch. We were passionate for the Lord and ready to do what He wanted us to do.

Don came home one day and told me that he thought we would be going to Senegal, Africa. He had seen an article, in French, from Senegal, Africa on the bulletin board at church and his spirit jumped. Your spirit is another way to sense the Holy Spirit. He didn't hear thoughts, he just knew. When Don said the words Senegal Africa, I immediately thought **SENEGAL AFRICA.** I did not tell him, but I was a bit skeptical. The very next day I was at work. I had the thought to go swimming at a seminary Don had graduated from. I didn't really want to go. It was February and I just wasn't in the mood. I knew that thought was from God, so I called Don and we went. Don was in the hot tub. He was telling some people his vision for Africa. When he told them, they said, "See those people in the water they are from Senegal Africa."

I instantly told God. "I got it God." God has a way of showing us when it's Him that's at work. We met the two people and of course, they were very nice. The first thing I asked them was "Do you have a picture of Senegal?" They did. It was on the coast and it was beautiful. God doesn't give us anything that is too difficult for us. 1st Corinthians 10:13 "God is faithful; he will not let you be tempted beyond what you can bear. But when you are tempted, he will also provide a way out so that you can endure it. He means it. We met with them several times and they went on to Rhode Island to be married. Don continued to keep in touch with them. They did get married and were getting ready to go back to Senegal. Don told them we would try to come to Senegal in July of 93. There was one problem. We didn't have the money to go. God always says do not worry about. Philippians 4:6-7 "Don't worry about anything, instead, pray about everything. Tell God what you need, and thank him for all he has done. Then you will experience God's peace, which exceeds anything we can understand. His peace will guard your hearts and minds as you live in Christ Jesus."

This is how we went to Senegal. The company I worked for did a cost reduction project for all salaried employees. People would develop teams that would think of ways to save money and they would turn in these cost reduction ideas into the corporate office. There was one problem, I could not think of any way the company could save money. But, there was a man in Chicago who put me on his team and his idea was picked for the cost reduction program. His plan would save the company a lot of money. When I found out my team had been picked, I was so excited. I thought my family could go to Disney World. One day God gave me this thought. "**What about Africa.**" I said, "I get it Lord." I called to see if we could get airfare to Africa using the coupons we would receive. They said there was airfare but it was only to Europe. Before I found out about the lack of airfare, I called to see if there were any hotels in Senegal. There was a resort there in Dakar which is the capital city of Senegal. When I was placing the order with the resort, I mentioned that we were missionaries. They told me that there was nude swimming on the beaches at the resort. That would have been a dilemma for Don except for the fact that God was totally in the situation. I found out that if we reserved the resort, we could get the airfare. After everything had been ordered (hotel and airfare) for May of 93, we got a letter from the resort saying they would not be opened until July of 93. We got our certificates back and we stayed the entire time with our Senegalese friends. We didn't even have to stay in a nude bathing location. Who would have thought that Corporate America would have sent us to Senegal Africa?

Our day came. We were off to Senegal. The air trip took twenty-two hours. We were so excited, it didn't seem that long. We flew to Chicago, then to London, then to Paris and finally to Senegal. We only got to see those countries from the air because our next planes immediately took off. We still got to see more than we would have. The grass is so much greener across the Atlantic. The Sahara Desert is bigger than you can image. I didn't think we would ever get across it. We only took $300 because we didn't have much money to spend. That was OK. But we didn't know that we would need it at the end of our trip.

We stayed in Senegal for three weeks and what a three weeks. The third day there, I realized we didn't have hot water. It didn't make a bit of difference to me.

When God's in it, everything is just fine. Our friend took us to the isle of Goree'. That is the location the slaves were brought before being sent to America. It was a terrible place. There were doors that opened to the ocean. Those poor slaves were jammed into the rooms like sardines. Places like that do open your eyes to the terrible mistreatment of people.

Michel's Family

Bread from Africa – Fresh every morning

Goats for sale

It was so neat to be able to walk and buy bread every morning. The bread was French bread and it was so good and fresh. The vendors would have pictures of the meat they were selling. One picture looked like they were selling dog. How gross is that. Later I found out, they were selling goat. That was better. One day Don and I went for a walk. On the walk there was a monkey outside a house on a chain. I was enjoying playing with the monkey. It had quite a pleasant character until it tried to bite me. We left right after that. No more playing with the monkey.

We got to visit our missionary's uncle. He had a very nice house and beautiful plants and fruits. They served us lunch and it was like a feast. They were so warm and welcoming. We had a great time. We also met other relatives. They all spoke French. I didn't know a thing they were saying. Once again, it didn't bother me a bit. I was in Africa.

Before we left on the trip, the Lord had shown Don something about water. He wasn't sure what God meant. He might have meant reconditioning the water or just finding it. We just didn't know. We decided to go to the city and get a bus to take us to the outskirts of the town. Maybe we could talk to the leader of the area. After we got to town, I decided that I was not going on this venture. The buses were old, no hotels, yuck. I would have to take a bus back to his house by myself. It didn't look good for me, but I was not worried. Finally, our friend said: "Donald, I will do anything for you, but I have to be back at church on Thursday." It was now Tuesday. Don made the right decision. He decided to pray. Here we were in the capital city of Senegal, Dakar. It was a big metropolis. There was one thing different in this city and New York. People lined the street selling there wares. There was hardly any room to walk. It was very sad. It seemed weird to pray outside in Dakar. People walking by probably thought we were crazy. As soon has Don had prayed, our friend took us to a lady that works on water projects in Africa. She called Assembly of God missionaries, Baptist missionaries, and a district pastor who was a native of the country. She made arrangement for us to stay at their homes each weekend. She would take us to the place and we would ride the bus home. What an experience.

WALKING WITH THE LORD – WHAT A WAY TO GO

The Assembly of God missionaries we stayed the weekend with

The first weekend, we went to the Assembly of God missionary's home. We went with the missionary to a street where the movie **Jesus** was being shown. Yes, right on the street. You wouldn't ever see that in America. The movie was in French, but that didn't matter to me. I was in Africa. Wow! Wow! Wow! The next day was Sunday. Don went with the missionary to church services with the tribes. They rang a tire ream to tell the tribal people they had arrived. One little boy couldn't walk. He had been given a penicillin shot that had hit his nerve and paralyzed him. That happens quite a lot in Africa. He was beating the drum. He was happy. He didn't let his impairment bother him. People in Africa don't need a lot to make them happy. The children have very few toys. One little child had a truck that was made out of wire and the tires were carved out of wood. The toy was just fine for the child. I didn't see any other toys anywhere. I imagine our kids would be very bored with that few toys.

Beverly laying on the hammock in Africa

Wire rim to call people to church

Church members

Don and the termite hill

While Don was gone, I stayed at the house and read a book in a hammock. I couldn't believe I was in Africa relaxing in a hammock. One thing Don and I were amazed about was the termite hills. They were as tall as us. Don and I were also shown wells that were running out of water. While I was at the missionary's house, I realized they did not have running water. That was easy; you just pour water in the toilet. The water and other materials flush right down. We do have a tendency to make things hard, don't we? When we left the missionaries home, we realized how simple life can be when you're walking with the Lord and depending on him. We left there in amazement.

The next weekend, we went to the Baptist missionary's home. It was very cozy. The spirit of God flowed in it. The night we came, a native tribal person had died. Don was privileged enough to get to go to the funeral. In Africa, some of the people go to extremes in grieving for the dead person. They holler, they moan, they scream. It is terrible. It goes on for day and days and days and days. It can demonic. It's one area of spiritual depravity that needs to be stopped. When Don and our host got home, we had a wonderful meal. It was in the Senegalese tradition. They brought one bowl of fish and rice. Yes, one. We all ate out of the same bowl. It's not as bad as you think. You just pick your spot, imagine a piece of pie, and eat. It was very tasty.

I found out that I made a big mistake when we went to Africa. I took shorts. In Africa, shorts means you're a women of ill repute. I surely didn't want to step on any toes. I was given a dress to wear. It worked out quite nice. One time God showed me that **there is not one mistake on earth that can not be corrected**. My apparel was a good example of that.

The next day, we took a tour of the wells there in Senegal. A lot of them were running out of water. They have bags that are released down into the well and then pulled up. It takes a lot of strength to pull the bags up. A lot of the wells do not have sanitary water. There is a lot of work to be done there. Nothing is impossible with God.

The next weekend we went to visit the district pastor's tribes. The first tribe was very nice. It had a well. The people could only draw from the well at certain times of the day, but it was water. They had a garden. A garden is very unusual because of the lack of water. They had a school. The little children were all sitting in rows learning all that they could. What a difference from our schools. A one room building with plain walls, no blackboard, wooden benches was all that they had. But, they still had a school. By the way, they were building a restroom. That was their first one. Can you imagine that? I got my leaf and went and used it even if it wasn't finished.

Baptist missionaries and home of believers

Well

Bottom of well

Water holding tank

WALKING WITH THE LORD – WHAT A WAY TO GO

Water trough

Village people of Mboutour

Then the district pastor took us to another village, Mboutour, which was further back in the bush. As we were traveling down the road, we saw great big Baobab trees. The district pastor told us that when the chief of the tribe died, he was buried in the trunk of the tree. I surely never heard of that. When we came to the tribe, there were a lot of tribe's people. They received us with great love. They started bringing their benches then we were told that the district pastor was giving a talk on God's love. He said: **"If God takes care of the sparrow, how much more will he take care of you"**. Then they told us that these people walk 4 miles everyday just to get water. We, first hand, discovered the true destitution of these people. There was a lady behind us who was grinding millet for their dinner. We don't truly know what hard work is, do we. Don and I didn't know what we could do to help these people, but we knew we wanted to help them.

We had brought our lunch, so we went into a Finnish Lutheran missionary's hut to eat. I thought they were Finished Lutherans. What a dork I was. We had gotten through about half of our meal, when the tribe's people brought us a bowl of fish and rice. They once again served the fish and rice out of one bowl and everyone eats from it. I thought of it as a piece of pie and tried to eat within my piece. Then another tribe's person brought us another bowl of fish and rice. They were willing to give us all they had. There are no words to explain what happened. It must be God's love spilling out from them. When we were leaving the tribe, one of the tribe's people brought me some Bissap leaves. They are used to make juice. It was very good. These people were very giving, selfless, and kind. The African country was burying a water pipe that would extend their source of water to the many tribes. The pipe was going to stop before it reached the village of Mboutour. God always knows the ending even though we don't. The village did get a faucet, but the tribe is so big, it did not service the outer sections. Now all they have to do is pull the water with a wagon to the rest of the tribe.

Our trip ended and Don and I were ready to go home with so many wonderful memories. We had taken about $300 dollars for our trip. Can you imagine that a trip to Africa only cost us $300. We did have one problem, but to God it really wasn't. When we got to the airport, we had $27 left. I wanted to give it to Michel, but Don said no, we might need it. We were checking in our baggage and it was going to cost about $250. We didn't realize that our luggage was over the limit because it wasn't over when we left DFW. I turned around and there was a Visa station. Boy could I relate to those Visa commercials saying that you could use Visa anywhere. We got by that one. We said goodbye to our entourage and started to leave for the plane. There was a table with a man sitting at it right before we went to the plant. He said, "Airport tax - $40". I turned around and the Visa station had closed. Oh Boy. Michel was gone. He didn't have a phone. What were we going to do? Don back tracked, talking to everyone he had talked to before, hoping that someone could help us. Everyone spoke French so it was a little hard to talk even though Don knew French. This is one time, we forgot to pray. How could we have forgotten to pray. Where did we think we would get without God. God is so good that sometimes he answers our prayer before we ask. This is one time he did. The last man Don talked to took us back over to the Tax man. He told him something and we gave the man our $27 and he let us through. How great is our God. We continued to support Michel and hear of his progress. **God is good – All the time.**

As you can see, my life has been wonderful with its ups and downs. The funny thing is my downs were like ups. Yes it was a little hard, but when God is always with you, nothing is so bad. I thank God right now for everything he has done in my life and continues to do.

Here is the down side. Don loved to hunt. He taught his son the same. Brad was 13. Don had just bought his son a gun for Christmas of 2000. He got his present a little early so they could go hunting for Thanksgiving. Don and Brad left on Friday morning and were due home Sunday night. Sunday night around, 8 p.m., a policeman came to door and told me that Brad had shot his Dad and killed him. I can not explain that feeling. So many thoughts were going through my mind. I even asked the policeman if they were sure it was Don. Krista immediately sobbed with grief. You see, Don had adopted her and he was the only Daddy she knew. It was like my whole life was over, but I knew it wasn't. I had my kids to think of and especially my boy who was 4 hours away. I knew that I didn't want to drive 4 hours to get my son, so I asked if there was anyone in Jefferson that could meet me halfway. There was a police officer there who was also a pastor and he did meet us in Tyler. Everything would work out because God was in it from the start. I called my older daughter, Lynn, and she told me that a friend saw 4 angels around Brad at the accident. "Wow!"

I asked the police officer if I could call Brad. He got Brad on the phone. He immediately started crying. The first thing I said to him was that it wasn't his fault. He said his uncles and aunt in Louisiana were going to be mad at him. I told him that they would understand that he was just 13 years old and didn't know all the rules. The sky was getting darker, and Brad thought his Dad went up the hill, but he didn't. He was even with him, but quite a way away. Brad saw something move and he shot. His Dad was wearing camouflage and Brad thought it was a deer. When he got over to the dead body, it was his Dad. His Dad died in 15 seconds, but Brad didn't know it. He gave his Dad CPR for a long time, not knowing his Dad was already dead. He had to wait with his Dad until the ambulance came. While he was waiting, he prayed "God, you raised Lazarus. Now raise my Dad." But, it wasn't God's time for Don to be raised from the dead. It was time for Don to go to Heaven to be with God, Jesus, and his departed family members and friends. If Don had not been a born again Christian, he would have gone to hell. You see, we had something to be happy about, but we couldn't see it for our grief. 1 Thessalonians 4:13 Brothers and sisters, we do not want you to be uninformed about those who sleep in death, so that you do not grieve like the rest of mankind, who have no hope." I never got mad at God, Don, or Brad. What a Godly blessing. That was a battle I didn't have to fight.

It almost seemed simultaneous but, after the police officer left our house, a large group of neighbors were at my front door. The Frost Baptist preacher, we didn't even go to their church, Krista's boyfriend's family and many others were there. Krista had gotten on the phone and called many people. They didn't care if it was late or not. It was like I didn't have to do anything. Everyone knew what to do and did it. We got in a circle and prayed. What a blessing. I soon found out that the preacher and his wife from our church were coming over to take us to Tyler. Now, we were on our way to get Brad. On the way to Tyler, millions of thoughts went through my head. How will I keep from crying, when I talk to Brad. How will

I comfort Brad? What kind of counseling will Brad need? How is Krista going to do? What can I do to help her? But most of all, I was praying knowing that God could give me the words for my kids and help me know what to do.

Well, I now had a 13 year old boy which was my responsibility to bring up. Remember he was a very spirited boy and sometimes I didn't know what to do with him. I prayed a lot. It was only through the prayers of loving people that Brad eventually got it and was saved. Don't give up on your kids, just keep praying and stay in touch with them. At first it wasn't too hard to raise Brad. Krista was away at college and Brad was the only one at home. I set guidelines. He knew when he was should be home and most of those times he made it. Sometimes I got in the car and went looking for him and found him. When Brad got to be about 17, things were changing and I didn't even know it. It's called marijuana. He started smoking it with the kids in the neighborhood and drinking liquor didn't help. We didn't have major problems, but it was an underlying issue. He graduated from High School and got accepted to junior college. He moved in with some guys and started living very loosely with the sex, marijuana, and liquor. They had a party one night and the police came. Brad was under age and got a ticket for liquor. One night he was hanging out with some kids and went upstairs to lie down. There was a problem downstairs and someone called the police. The police knocked on Brad's door, came in, and found marijuana in the bookshelves. He was put in jail for that one. I could have talked and talked and talked to him about these occurrences, but it wouldn't have affected him. All I could do was pray. I found out later how important consistent pray is. He did always have a job which I thought was great. I just didn't know everything that was going on.

Brad got accepted to a university about two hours away. Brad had a good job and I thought he could transfer his job there. He didn't think it would happen. He was looking through it with fleshly eyes. (the world's eyes) I prayed and asked the Lord to help in this area. He sure did because he was able to transfer his job to the new location.

Brad wanted to be a Science teacher. There was one problem - Math. Brad just didn't like Math, but he tried it anyway. He started trying to get happy. He found out that he just couldn't. The next step was marijuana. One day, I was trying to find Brad. I don't know why I was trying to find him with him 2 hours away and in college, but I was. I even had my daughter Krista calling people. Brad liked those games that you can play with people all over the country. They found a girl way up North that he had been playing with. My good friend even came over to be with me. We talked to the police officer whose son was good friends with Brad and he said he would find him. Sure enough, He came over the next morning and told me Brad was in jail. Off my friend and I went to the jail. The first thing Brad said when we got there was "I'm going to join the Navy". He just didn't know what he could do to turn his life around. We had to pay a lot of money to get him out of this one and it would be on his record. He was kicked out of Sam Houston University.

During this time, I found out Brad was saying ugly things about God to different people. He was a mess. He decided to move back home and get away from the kids on drugs and liquor. Thank goodness he decided to move back home instead of living with someone else. I didn't realize it but Brad was at rock bottom. He had lost everything including himself. He was very confused about God, the Bible and everything that went with it. All I could do was pray. Watch how prayer and God worked it all out. Brad had been home a couple of weeks. He walked up to me and said "Mom, I have a joy that only God could give me". Wow! I said to myself, I don't believe this. You see I had been praying for a lot of years for Brad's salvation and that he would meet a Godly girl. I knew that Brad had a will of his own and God would not overrule that. Brad was so disgusted about all that he had done and didn't know what was left. He said," God if you really exist, show me". Brad had no reason to be happy but all of a sudden he felt this overwhelming amount of joy. He realized God had given him that joy. His life totally changed that day. In two weeks he met a Godly girl. They fell in love and got married. They have two children and work in a home for abused and hurting children. Now, they can serve God and help children know that there is a living God, His Son, Jesus

Christ, and the Holy Spirit who loves them and will help them in many ways.

I'm going to back track and show you how God can do miracles in your life that are beyond explanation. When Brad applied for the job in the children's home, he had been arrested twice. In order to be hired, Brad had to write two essays. One was why he went to jail and the other one was why he went to jail twice. Because of the wrong things Brad had done in his short lifetime, he should not have been hired. God can do all things. Nothing is impossible with God. God proved this when he allowed Brad to get hired under those circumstances. God knows our capabilities and gives us many opportunities to serve him. He gives us another chance even when the world doesn't.

God continues to do many miracles in my life. My house had a big problem. It needed to be leveled. I used Don's insurance money to get it fixed. I paid the guy $14,000 and he left me high and dry. He dug big holes around the house and off he went. I was really mad at myself for two days. I said to myself, you can be mad at yourself or you can pray. I decided to pray. When I prayed, I received God's peace about it and kind of forgot the circumstance. Three months later, a man owed a man at our church $25,000. This man leveled houses. He allowed the man to level my house and told the man his debt was gone.

When Don died, his best friend, in Louisiana, was led by the Lord to help me. When I needed property tax money, he sent it to me. When Brad wanted to go to college, he sent me $600 a month. Yes $600 a month. He is now sending $700 a month and Brad's not even in college. What a blessing from God. I had 2 cars each having about 140,000 miles. He bought his secretary's mom's van and gave it to me. I was taking my Mom to my sister's house and the transmission went out. I called him and told him what had happened. He said, "I'll get you a car you can depend on. Pick out a car between $18,000 and $21,000 and I will send you a check. I did and he did. That was the first new car I had in over 24 years. What a treat for me. When that car got old, he sent me money for a new one. I needed a new roof. He sent me $8,700. My air conditioner went out. He sent me $4,000. God told me that he does a lot of miracles for people and most of them are done through other people. Don's friend is proof of that.

It took me a long time to know what God's calling was for me. Here it is. I do volunteer work at a juvenile correctional facility and get to talk to the boys about God. At the end of my hour, one of the boys wanted to talk to me. He said he was a Satanist. I didn't even know what to say to him. Sometimes God gives us the words and this time he did. Towards the end of our conversation, he told me he wanted to be saved. Wow. We prayed the salvation prayer and the next two weeks went well. The third week he told me he was hearing screams in the night. You do know who that was. It was Satan and his demons. Satan did not want this boy to live for God. I got a prayer to pray against Satan from our Jail leader at church. The boy said he was still hearing the Satanic yelling. I prayed a different prayer with him and he was still hearing the screams. The next week I took matters into my own hands. I anointed the boy and his cell with anointing oil from Jerusalem. The other boys also wanted to be prayed over with the anointing oil. They were afraid the demons would jump on them. The next week the boy said, "It's working". He did not here the screaming any more.

Another thing that has happened in my life is so wonderful. My friend, Kathy Holmes, and I have been going out to eat once a week for 17 years. We talk about God, pray for each other, pray for others and watch God do His thing. My friend and I were not friends at all until God miraculously put us together. A lot of people want to know how to hear from God. Since I know how, I like to tell them. My friend knows the Bible very well and can help them know the scriptural aspect of God, Jesus and the Holy Spirit. With the help of God we really get their attention. Many people have been saved (even at restaurants) through God's anointing power.

If you are not putting God first in your life and living the way you want, as I did, think about it. God is the sovereign God of the universe and knows you better then you know yourself. He can turn your life into a wonderful way to live as he did for my son. Just pray to God and ask Jesus into your heart. God will guide your every step if you just let him.

Someday I would like to tell my story in churches. If God wants me to, nothing can stop me.

Would you like to know why I wrote this book. I'll tell you. I was telling a perfect stranger my story. She said, "You ought to write a book". This statement was totally out of my box. Two weeks later, the same thing happened. I told this stranger, her statement was totally out of my box. I went home that night and prayed, "God, if you want me to write this book, give me the title. Immediately I got this thought "WALKING WITH THE LORD - WHAT A WAY TO GO". Isn't God Grand.

About the Author

BEVERLY K. PLAUCHÉ is just an ordinary person. She does know one thing: she loves God, Jesus, and the Holy Spirit very much. If it weren't for those three, her husband and kids would not be where they are today.

She received her bachelor's degree in business administration from Baylor University. She did not get a degree in writing. If God wants you to write a book, that is immaterial.

She has had two jobs in her lifetime: a financial manager for a manufacturing company and a teacher. Those two professions don't really go together, but they worked. She is now retired, and through God's miraculous power, she lives very comfortably.

Through the thirty-four years of walking with the Lord, her life has been very exciting and passionate. God sure does things a lot differently than we expect him to, but that's what makes life thrilling. Sometimes, we have hard times in our lives, but if we are living for the Lord, everything will be okay.

www.ingramcontent.com/pod-product-compliance
Lightning Source LLC
LaVergne TN
LVHW020446080526
838202LV00055B/5358